ancient history

Rhyanna Potter

BookLeaf
Publishing

India | USA | UK

Presentation by *BookLeaf Publishing*

Web: www.bookleafpub.com

E-mail: info@bookleafpub.com

ISBN: 9789358317916

First edition 2024

*My muses, past loves, lost lives, and many
selves.*

ACKNOWLEDGEMENT

Thank you to my aunt and adopted mother, who believed in me enough to help me get this book of poetry published.

PREFACE

This is an exercise of faith, a trust fall, and a scream into the void.

unhinged

i don't know how else to say it
i miss you
but i'll never forgive you

the stages of grief
are like morning sickness
you feel them all at once, all day

losing you hurts just as bad
as any lover i've ever known

history and lessons

2

You were history
And lessons
Big and small blessings
Unsolved mysteries
Spaghetti westerns

ghosts

abandoned reciprocity
worse than the chemistry
that seeps from the history
we carry on our backs
the late night panic attacks
over the ghost of your hands like track
marks on my bone marrow
vessels too narrow
to carry love this thick

les miserables

i'm fantine
im eponine
i'm lying, dying face down in the dirt
incredible how this continues to hurt
how do you manage to flirt yet skirt
any word of substance

midas

getting to know you has been like
unclenching a fist, finger by finger
over the course of years
you opened up, and held me
in the palm of your hand
and closed it again

atrophy

6

the act of creation
when your dreams have been taken
a few too many times, is akin
to flexing an atrophied muscle.

stranger

i am a stranger in a strange land
one that few can understand
i carry the sins of my father in my open hands
cloaked in a shroud of his reprimands
opportunities fall like figs, flow like time's sand
through my fingers, regret often lingers
in my doorway, fumbling her keys as she stands
to leave me yearning again, my friend,
and i finally begin to comprehend
that the more we change, the more we end
up staying the same, and isn't it just a shame
you've become a stranger, just a name
in my phone;
when i used to call you home.

hoarding

8

hoarding runs in my family
the great depressions lingers in our genes
and scarcity clings like spiderwebs
in my grandmother's heart
unclenching your fist and letting go is an art
we have yet to master
and i am a hoarder of memory
stories with a glint of anything shimmery
a glimmer, a crumb of love, anything that proves
i was here
and you saw my face
even for a moment.

i asked god to send a swordsman

i'm not much of a writer
but for you i would ride or die
my pen is mightier, has more power
than any sword you could pin me down with
but i would have lived and died by your word
if only you had given me a third of
the devotion i had for you

sitting on the fence

I never had the words to convince
you: "please commit to
me, come here to me,"
but
all you gave me, was silence
so blinding, so intense;
don't know where the time went
and the memory makes me wince -
Your hands and eyes and scents
And
I see your face in God, in frankincense,
guess it's you I gave up for Lent
But
I never meant to,
Bring an end to, I'd get off this fence
for you, haven't been the same since
you, left your fingerprints
on me, there's no defense
for me, can we go back to
back then, to when, to past-tense
before I said goodbye out of self-defense?

not the type

I'm not the type, not the girl
you dreamed of
I'm not the girl anyone
planned or asked for
My father was the first
man I disappointed, and
I've been wrapping myself
in food and sadness since
So when I'm unwanted,
Kissed and
Dismissed by you,
It's a familiar place
I keep coming back to
Because I understand how
I look, how I sound, and
I wouldn't want me either.

pedestal

12

you looked better from a distance
on the pedestal i placed you on
before i could see the cracks in your foundation
and the holes in your logic
from way up there you looked so perfect
carved from stone, untouchable
up close i saw your freckles and your sins
and a part of me wished to
put you back up there again

stalemate

i no longer create
all i do is ache and
wait for the pain to abate
rotting in bed while i conflate
the agony of nostalgia
with love

basket of broken eggs

waking up from another nightmare
i would say it's not fair but
what does a discerning universe care
for my yearning, as the world keeps turning
round on its axis, guess i'll just need to practice
projecting a calmness i don't feel, that isn't real
just to keep on moving

burning

Over the course of my life
I have found that my devotion flickers
Like flares from a small dying sun.
I am bright
And hot
And then I am nothing, forever.
I am
Half-empty notebooks of
Half-hearted poetry and prose
With half-watched TV shows.
But
There are no half-loved people
Because your love is gasoline
And I am a carelessly tossed cigarette
Still wet from the edges of your mouth
And I am burning
Like the tiniest star in the universe
Big enough to warm only you.
But I am burning.

Alexithymia

I never was much good with words,
Or spinning tales like yarn in
The tiny pink blanket that Ruth made for me.
In front of a crowded room, I have
To take my glasses off
Just to remember what I have to say.
It's worse when I'm with you,
My jaw locks up like I got tetanus
From the rust in my pickup lines.

Speechless in love or in anger, or
When asked a question in class
About the meaning of my art.

I don't know, okay. It means nothing,
Everything to me, these marks
On a page, the words in
My throat, stuck there like
The grape i choked on when i was four.

Sitting on the bed as you scream,
Begging for an adult reply,
And i have no voice to tell
You that I can't.

Because my communication skills
Stopped growing with me when i was
Fourteen, even though my vocabulary
Expanded.
And i'm sorry that my silence drives you mad,
If I could, I would unhinge myself and
All my responses would tumble out,
Eloquent and shining and hot
As the water we shower in.

I would open myself to you, guide
Your gingers into the wetness of
My lungs and liver,
Maybe you would find something
Worth keeping down in my core,
Something that explains all my
Performance problems.

flashbacks

I still carry thoughtful gift ideas
For people I hope to never see again.
Entirely too much precious space
goes to waste remembering
the color of your favorite author's
typewriter, or lines from your favorite
best/worst movie.
Sometimes my body reacts before
my brain has to jog to catch up
To find the right reasons for the
tightness in my chest, the tremor in my hands.
I'm slowly undoing the damage
Rolling back the years, but I can't
Reset the clock or unremember
Your fists and the hate on your face.
I am who I am and you're a choice
I made, and this too I shall include,
But sometimes I wish so hard for
Your death that I feel my heart may crack
Open and spill out your favorite color
Or the precise shade of your hair in the
summer (before you bleached it) or
All the cruel things you ever said to me
Will pour out and then you'll be sorry.

salusa secundus

i love the deep sea for the same reason
i love the desert
because anything that grows there
had to work for it
maybe i should
love myself for the same reason

seamstress

20

i'm sewing up my seams,
it seems that's for the best
despite how i lay awake at night, chasing rest
and maybe i truly am blessed,
even if i can't see it yet
wrestling with all my regret
will i ever be able to forget
the tears i cried, the words you said?

the self

my sense of self has always been shaky,
like a suspension bridge missing a few cables
shaky like my hands on your chest for the first
time,
shaky like too many days fasting
my birth chart says my core wound is in
creativity
so how can i begin to create a solid self out of
all these shambles, how can i build an identity
when i can barely craft a sentence?
and it's not just matrescence
that's robbed me of myself
it's been a lifetime of "we'll figure it out"
the tarot says it'll all work out, but
how do i know who is on the other side
and how can i trust in the divine
(of any kind)
when i don't even trust myself?

my daughter

i hope i've done enough for my daughter
to prevent her becoming cannon fodder
for someone's dusty son.
i hope over the years, i've taught her
enough to love herself more
than any man ought to.

www.ingramcontent.com/pod-product-compliance
Lightning Source LLC
LaVergne TN
LVHW051248200726
843510LV00011B/1739